COLORES MEXICAN INTERIORS

SANDY BAUM

Schiffer Publishing Ltd®
4880 Lower Valley Road, Atglen, PA 19310

I0799352

Other Schiffer Books by Sandy Baum:
San Miguel's Mexican Exteriors. ISBN: 978-0-7643-3004-9. $39.99
San Miguel's Mexican Interiors. ISBN: 978-0-7643-2947-0. $14.95
Mexican Gardens & Patios, ISBN: 978-0-7643-3267-8. $29.99

Copyright © 2009 by Sandy Baum
Library of Congress Control Number: 2009924946

All rights reserved. No part of this work may be reproduced or used in any form or by any means—graphic, electronic, or mechanical, including photocopying or information storage and retrieval systems—without written permission from the publisher.

The scanning, uploading and distribution of this book or any part thereof via the Internet or via any other means without the permission of the publisher is illegal and punishable by law. Please purchase only authorized editions and do not participate in or encourage the electronic piracy of copyrighted materials.

"Schiffer," "Schiffer Publishing Ltd. & Design," and the "Design of pen and ink well" are registered trademarks of Schiffer Publishing Ltd.

Designed by John P. Cheek
Cover design Bruce Waters
Type set in Lydian Csv BT/Adobe Jenson Pro

ISBN: 978-0-7643-3301-9
Printed in China

Schiffer Books are available at special discounts for bulk purchases for sales promotions or premiums. Special editions, including personalized covers, corporate imprints, and excerpts can be created in large quantities for special needs. For more information contact the publisher:

Published by Schiffer Publishing Ltd.
4880 Lower Valley Road
Atglen, PA 19310
Phone: (610) 593-1777; Fax: (610) 593-2002
E-mail: Info@schifferbooks.com

For the largest selection of fine reference books on this and related subjects, please visit our web site at **www.schifferbooks.com**
We are always looking for people to write books on new and related subjects. If you have an idea for a book please contact us at the above address.

This book may be purchased from the publisher.
Include $5.00 for shipping.
Please try your bookstore first.
You may write for a free catalog.

In Europe, Schiffer books are distributed by
Bushwood Books
6 Marksbury Ave.
Kew Gardens
Surrey TW9 4JF England
Phone: 44 (0) 20 8392 8585; Fax: 44 (0) 20 8392 9876
E-mail: info@bushwoodbooks.co.uk
Website: www.bushwoodbooks.co.uk

Contents

RAVENNA

Acknowledgments

San Miguel de Allende has been my home for over four years, and in that time I've made many friends who have been supportive of my endeavor to bring to the public photography books on Mexican style. Working on this book, as with others about San Miguel, has been a joy and a pleasurable experience, mostly because of the new friends and acquaintances I was fortunate to meet along the way. I hope you, the reader, enjoy this journey behind closed doors and walls that line the streets, a journey to which the typical visitor will not be invited.

This book would not have been possible without the editorial input of friends and neighbors: Betsy January, probably my most vocal editor and critic; Alegria Skully who, with her husband, Mike Skully, have spent hours poring over my text; Phil Jeffrey, an English major when she was in college, keeps correcting both my English as well as my poor Spanish; Leona Camp who worked on some of my earlier text, and Nancy Newton, when she is in town between her world travels.

Susan Page was one of my early moral supporters with her comment, "Do you know how lucky you are?" Lulu Torbet was also a supporter who volunteered to go over my early material. A special thanks goes to my two editors at Schiffer Publishing, Ltd., Nancy Schiffer and Tina Skinner. Without their patience and foresight, this book may not have made it into your hands. And finally, a great big thanks to all the homeowners who were kind enough to open their doors each Sunday for the House & Garden tour sponsored by the Biblioteca Publica, a weekly fund-raising event for the many programs that exist at the library, programs aimed to educate the Mexican children of San Miguel. I thank you all.

ARMAS DEL
ALMIRANTE
DON RAMON BONIFAZ

Introduction

Enter into a little-known world of magic, mystery and color behind the walls of some of the most exclusive living areas in San Miguel de Allende. This is a world created by each of the homeowners with a bent for the exotic and different, where no two interiors are the same, and with all the variety and creative effort brought to bear; always with the added ingenuity and input of the local Mexican workers.

One of the defining elements of the Mexican way of life is the uninhibited use of color, provided by a palette of vibrant pinks, yellows, blues and reds. Mexico has always been a country of color, even before Cortez discovered New Spain (Mexico). The cochineal, a tiny insect that feeds off cacti, when dried out, produces vibrant reds through the use of various juices. Natural yellows come from marigold petals and orange from the Annatto tree berries.

San Miguel is no different, with its kaleidoscope of color. Turn a corner, walk the canyons formed by the narrow streets with building walls on either side, or fly overhead in a hot air balloon and color stands out everywhere you look. Historically, Mexicans displayed color as part of their heritage, giving one a sense of joy, of being alive. Colors inside the homes reflect the owners' personalities...you can tell a lot about a person by the colors with which they choose to surround themselves.

In many towns throughout Mexico, houses still retain blank exteriors facing the street, some with an occasional window. However, beyond these canyon-forming walls, one is exposed to interiors alive with rainbows of color. Where the front of the house may be one story, once inside the entrance, a visitor might be exposed to two or more stories, probably with a rooftop terrace and a fantastic view of the downtown skyline.

The architecture of the houses in the original center of town reflects an era when Mexico was at an early peak in its history, when most of these buildings were extravagant homes built by some of the country's most famous families. Now they house only commercial or public venues. The rich quality of the architecture, however, has not diminished with time.

Color is only one of the many ingredients that reflect the Mexican way of life that forms a bond with the human spirit. Here the air is clear, the sunlight is bright with sharp shadows, and the sky is a vibrant cobalt blue.

CHAPTER

1

Doors

Cantera stone surrounds this simple, double-leaf door with various metal embellishments.

This double entry door, set in a massive stone framework, is both a pedestrian door and a garage door.

A scorched-finish look to an otherwise healthy pair of doors surrounded by *cantera*.

This pair of wooden doors stands out with its half-round transom, radiating sun symbol, and visible door bell.

This contemporary double-leaf wooden door is set in a wooden frame. Notice that the two doors are not the same size. One side is fixed while the other is the entry door. The fixed door can be opened whenever a large object must pass through.

An oversized metal door with a design-in-place frame. The weight of this door necessitates using pivots at the top and bottom, in lieu of standard hinges.

A handmade, multi-paneled door with a simple door pull framed by *cantera*.

This entry is adjacent to a narrow walkway facing a two-story building to the south, causing very little sunlight to reach this entry wall. This full-height glass wall, with glass doors, provides much-needed light to the lowest house level.

A multi-faceted, wrought iron gate secures the outdoor entry while providing a see-through to visitors.

This tall double entry door with glass transom was designed for tall carriages. The *cantera* frame was added later.

Beyond the entry, past the open courtyard on the right, this door leads to the bedroom wing. The door on the left leads to the living room.

This ornately carved, double-entry door is a typical design by local master carvers. The opening has a center-designed stile, part of the fixed leaf, for a more secure pair of doors. The fixed leaf can be opened for the passage of large objects.

Privacy to the bedroom is provided by this pair of solid doors.

A window, designed to replicate the door, looks into the house. It is shorter than the doors, providing a window seat on the interior.

This slightly ajar door leads to the guest bathroom.

Glass provides additional light from the courtyard into the dining room.

A pair of small windows provides easy views into the kitchen and may help to forestall any possible accidents when coming and going.

This view of the double-leafed entry door is from the inside of the home. The door is made of multiple slats with a similarly designed transom. As with most doors of this weight and size, the standard number of hinges was doubled.

A beautiful stained glass insert is in this wooden entry door.

An elaborately carved door with a rounded frame on top.

A wooden entry door with transom is recessed within a tall arched front.

CHAPTER 2

Living Rooms

This is a comfortable living room with the fireplace center stage. *Saltillo* tile with area rugs is standard in many Mexican homes.

Equipal chairs and an *equipal* loveseat dominate this conversation area, while facing a locally made cabinet for the homeowners' folk art collection.

This comfortable seating area looks out on the adjacent patio, as seen in the mirror on the back wall.

Notice the elephant ladder in the far left corner. In India, riding elephants is a daily pastime, and the ladder is used to climb up onto the elephant's back, after which the ladder is brought up as well, collapsed, and carried along for the ride.

This living room adjoins the courtyard for easy entertaining.

Adjacent to the kitchen, this living room is convenient for entertaining. Notice the ship's ladder leading to the loft bedroom above the kitchen.

This three-piece sofa combination surrounds a locally made coffee table that uses old wooden flooring from an abandoned building as the top.

The black and white paint scheme goes well with the two grey *cantera* monkeys that hold up the fireplace mantel.

The light area rug sits on a warm parquet wooden floor. The colors are complementary, while the bookshelves warm this corner of the room.

In a room with white walls such as this, any color stands out, including those in the paintings on the walls.

The French doors with arched transoms allow exterior light to brighten this room, while the light painted walls create a larger-looking space.

This elegant living room has light-colored walls, sofas, and coffee table in sharp contrast to the rust-colored paint in the adjacent dining area.

Shades of yellow and pink are used with a green sofa. The dark coffee table offers strong contrast.

This image shows the adjacent dining room through a framed doorway with wooden lintel. Much-welcomed daylight streams from the courtyard.

The old chest serves double duty in this elongated living room with a curved, brick *boveda* ceiling.

The small tile in the fireplace opening sharply contrasts the *cantera* surround set amidst a green envelope. In another photo showing the ceiling in this room, the ceiling reveals a painted tile-look instead of the actual tiles.

This very large living space includes the dining area (not visible in this photo) and a massive fireplace. This family home was originally built by the *Patron* using fluted columns from a former church as the basis for the floor plan.

The massive coffee table with tree-sized legs in front of the *cantera* fireplace dominates this room.

This large, flowing, living space includes a dining area with a *cantera* floor.

Here the sofa and area rug are in sharp contrast to the marble fireplace surround. The *equipal* chairs have a softening effect on the hard *saltillo* tile floor.

The cane-backed sofa and chest contrast with the dark-stained *equipal* table and chairs. A *cantera* mantel is supported by two *cantera* columns.

CHAPTER

3

Kitchens

This colorful kitchen has a solid *talavera* tile countertop with a patterned backsplash and *saltillo* floor tile. The breakfast area is beyond the countertop return.

A breakfast area is part of this kitchen with *talavera* tile in a *medio-pañuelo* pattern on the counter and shelf edges.

This elongated kitchen has a corner sink and the return housing a dishwasher. Light *talavera* tile adorns the countertop with blue facing tiles. The breakfast nook is just to the right.

This compact kitchen has all the conveniences in spite of its size. Of course, *saltillo* tile aids in countertop clean-up. A breakfast nook is to the right and a pantry is beyond the island counter.

This small kitchen has a turquoise countertop adjacent to the dining and living areas that are just off the west-facing patio. French doors with arched transoms emit welcome natural light.

Bright blue *talavera* tile on the countertop has a blue horizontal facing edge and vertical columns frame the appliances. The backsplash is a different solid with a patterned edge.

A bright yellow panel above the burners accents the rust-colored kitchen walls. Black and white, diamond-patterned tiles on the backsplash contrast with the brown-stained cabinets.

There is no lack of storage space in this kitchen. Marble countertops and *cantera* flooring help to keep this kitchen clean.

The island with a center sink makes this an efficient kitchen with ample storage below and in wall cabinets beyond.

This bright, white kitchen has green patterned tile facing the countertop and as a kick space below the cabinets. A *boveda* ceiling and *saltillo* floor complete the room.

It was party time when this kitchen was photographed. This compact, well laid out kitchen waits for the dishwasher in the space used by a trash container. The solid, tan *talavera* tile goes well with the stained wooden cabinets.

A white-on-white kitchen with a wooden countertop on the island. The dark-stained flooring goes well with the appliances.

Black painted cabinets provide sharp contrast to the marbleized countertop in this kitchen with stainless steel fronts on the black appliances.

Another compact kitchen with stainless steel appliances and a *cantera* floor. The glass wall brightens this room.

In the all-white kitchen, the cabinet tops are great places for additional display space.

The dark stained cabinets provide strong contrast to the beige colored tile countertops. The copper hood reads well with the rust colored wall behind.

The blue *talavera* countertop facing and the double band surrounding the backsplash create a "saw tooth" pattern.

This well equipped kitchen has the massive oven-range built into one corner and the sink occupying the center island. The blue and white tile band accentuates the window, pantry door, and backsplash. With a large pantry beyond the double refrigerator, you don't see any wall cabinets.

This compact kitchen is surrounded by windows that emit a great deal of natural light.
The finish on the dark paver floor reflects the light well.

This photo and the next provide two views of a contemporary kitchen with black cabinets. The appliance fronts and range hood are stainless steel. This is a bachelor's pad designed by the owner.

Same kitchen as the previous photo.

CHAPTER

4

Dining Rooms

This dining area as well as the blue wall at the back are brighten by overhead skylights.

The red painted chairs go well with the flowers in the tablecloth.
The huge window beyond brings welcome daylight into this area.

Padded seating makes for more comfortable dining. The herringbone pattern on two *talavera* jars sitting in front of mirrors makes a bold statement.

A collector's antique table and chairs sit on an old Mexican-designed area rug.

This old carved table is protected with a sheet of glass on top. The carving matches the cabinet and the table used behind the green-patterned couch.

Simplicity personifies this bachelor's pad with a clean, contemporary look. The second level of a three-level home is shown, with the dining room, living room, and kitchen on a very narrow lot.

A breakfront cabinet, table, and chairs are hand-carved wood. The soft cushions are welcome for extended, sit-down dinners.

The glass-topped dining table and leather-backed chairs with colorful seats blend well with the glass-topped shelf against the back wall.

The red and white striped chairs complement the red and tan table runner. An old cabinet against the wall is a restored find from an earlier home.

The beautifully patterned cloth covering these dining room chairs is reminiscent of a bygone French era. The colors blend well with the painted walls

The stained *cantera* floor has a reflective finish. Carved cabinet doors were crafted at a local woodworking shop.

A glass top on an old door with ten separate panels makes an interesting table. It and the chairs rest on a Mexican area rug and herringbone-patterned *saltillo* tiles.

The dining table and tall, red and white cushioned chairs sit in a sea of grey *cantera* floor tiles. A large mirror with hand-tooled metal frame leans against the wall.

A red area rug focuses attention to the center of this otherwise light-colored room. The ceramic bowl centerpiece with blue striped edge and three pelicans was made in San Miguel.

Looking beyond the living area, a dining space has a continuous floor of *saltillo* tile that extends to an outdoor patio. Jars of various sizes line the far right wall. Two red pots adjacent to the credenza are from Michoacán.

The drop-leaf table and chairs with white seats were locally made, while the credenza was acquired during the owner's world travels. The area rug is a Mexican design.

A red faux-painted finish on the walls is outstanding. The arched doorways lead to the kitchen.

This cozy breakfast area just off the kitchen is flanked by doors and windows that provide ample natural light.

This dining area's round table and blue upholstered *equipal* chairs are in the *casita,* adjacent to the main house. A round area rug on *saltillo* tiles complements the layout.

A locally made wooden table with glass inserts and chairs with patterned cushions occupy the mustard-colored dining area with herringbone-patterned floor tiles.

This massive great room contains both the dining area and seating for the living space. Elegant grey upholstered chairs match the black-framed area rug. All the wood has the same dark finish.

The glass-topped table has a beveled edge. The table runner was acquired during the owners' distant travels.

CHAPTER 5

Bedrooms

An ornate headboard is a favorite style throughout Mexico. These bedroom walls have a faux finish.

The matching bedspread and area rugs add more than a touch of color.

A massive headboard defines this bed on a white, patterned rug. The corridor to the bathroom is paved with *saltillo* tiles.

The wooden beam ceiling is characteristic of early Mexican construction. Here, a tall four-poster bed has interesting designs in the headboard and footboard. The foot-locker on raised legs matches the colorful area rug below.

This bedroom shows a shuttered opening and two windows that provide light to brighten the room.

This is a cozy guest bedroom with two large windows that brighten the interior.

A dark cabinet matches the door frame as well as the beams above.

The green and orange sections of the wall are divided by a wainscot. Orange in the throw pillow and green throws match the wall.

This massive bed was locally made, with carved headboard and footboard.

This bedroom of an avid collector reflects his interests. The colorful round platters are part of a much larger collection and the four paintings are by the homeowner.

A beautiful Mexican textile bedspread with matching pillows adorns this bed in a niche with a stunning clamshell cove.

A wrought iron headboard fills the recess in this niche. Purple lamp shades on matching nightstands complement the colors in the bedspread and pillows.

The multi-colored fabric bedspread and dark green sham bring color to the bed. Hour-glass shaped *saltillo* floor tiles and the area rug complement the night stand fronts. Part of a fan collection hangs on the wall to the right.

The wall hanging, bedspread and area rug have complementing colors. The macaw sits idly by surveying the scene.

The handwork on these quilts is outstanding, as is the carved headboards on these twin beds. The colors of the green pillow are repeated in the area rug.

With multiple colors and patterns everywhere, where does the eye begin? From the original designed bright blue bed frame, the *talavera* platters, the yellow lamp with the white shade, and the painting above the headboard, one's eye is constantly roaming.

CHAPTER 6

Bathrooms

The *talavera* vase with peacock feathers picks up the colors in the two mirror frames above copper sinks and matching faucets.

The solid talavera countertop and backsplash has a ceramic rope trim piece.

The raised white sinks with black faucet finish are a nice contrast to the green tile countertop and backsplash and faux finished walls. The reflection in the mirror shows that the tile goes around the bathroom.

This countertop has a modified front to allow a larger bowl to be recessed within. The black faucet set is a nice contrast with the metal frame of the mirror, and twin sconces provide light and reflection. The diamond pattern on the backsplash is reflected in the bowl.

The triple mirrors reflect the window frame beyond. A black diamond pattern and a sea of oatmeal tile at the backsplash contrast nicely with the solid oatmeal color on the countertop.

This extensively used *talavera* flower design is similar to the Arabesque pattern. The clever use of this tile in varied positions is pleasing.

The drop-in copper sink is a nice color against the tan tiled countertop. The green grey tile on the walls is a soft contrast.

The extensive use of black and white tile makes an interesting design with the wainscot topped with the same tile and the sink continues the pattern.

A round tub set in the corner takes advantage of this small but bright bathroom with two windows. The *talavera* tile with bird border at the top of the tall wainscot is called "flight."

This bathroom has a green tile border above the wainscot. The gold frame of the mirror, black frame on the wall, and floor tile add color.

This small guest bathroom with corner cabinet has a nice color combination.

Warm wall color with matching tile give color contrast to the wall-to-wall mirrors and dark wood cabinets.

The sea-green countertop tile and brown floor tile complement the cabinets.

A copper tub is a nice feature of this spacious bathroom.

Midnight-blue tile surrounds a hand-painted sink recessed into the countertop.

This concrete countertop and base are faced with small white stones.

This countertop required a great deal of design planning. With one end on an angle, square tiles were not called for. Tile remnants were used to form an interesting pattern in two colors.

CHAPTER 7

Bathroom Details

Here a bright yellow sink is set into yellow tiles with a strip of wood trim finishing the countertop edge.

A yellow sink and rust-colored tile has a frame of textured brown tile around the entire room.

Red and black tiles in a fanciful design are inside a round shower. Several strategically placed slotted windows brighten the shower.

A more recent design innovation places the sink on the countertop. Here a rectangular bowl was chosen.

The glass-enclosed shower is lined with *cantera*. There is no aluminum frame around the glass and the hinges are in plain sight.

Built-in exposed shelves store towels and other items normally found in a medicine cabinet.

A pair of white bowls sit on the grey tiled countertop. With the faucet set into the rear wall above the bowls, an interesting design element was introduced above the backsplash, and the one-piece mirror was cut to fit.

A little bit of whimsy was introduced in the next three photos. Here is an undulating countertop following the bowl forms set on top of the counter.

The sinks in this one-piece, tapered countertop were recessed as the countertop was poured.

Two sinks were carved into the undulating countertop. Notice the hour-glass shaped mirror and the window at the left.

The interesting shape of the base cabinet has a bay front, while narrowing to allow a wider access to the tub.

A detail of a sink bowl on tiled countertop with backsplash. Small tiles are between the backsplash and the faucet set.

An interesting use of a wrought iron table with a pan top to receive the tile and recessed sink. The same square tiles are used on the wainscot in a diagonal pattern.

Another bright yellow and white bathroom with a white herringbone design running throughout. The yellow tile wainscot stands at 42 inches with a two-inch white cap.

The yellow and white motif continues. Notice the *boveda* ceiling as you make your way toward the shower.

Talavera tile border: Guia AV-15.

Detail of dark tile added to highlight the backsplash with a double quarter round on either side.

Detail of the quarter round with "Vaqueti."

A combination of various pieces brought together where the wainscot wraps two corners.

Detail.

Detail.

Detail.

Detail of special fish "Innovation."

CHAPTER 8

Stairways

An interesting design in sculpted concrete, this interior stairway leads to a loft bedroom.

A short outdoor flight leads to the utility area.

The treads on this interior flight are made of *cantera* for long life.

This curving stairway to the second floor has stained *cantera* treads and an interesting metal railing design.

This curving stairway is covered in ceramic tiles with ceramic bull nose treads. Notice the wrought iron railing.

This contemporary stairway to a loft was a recent addition.

The tile-faced risers provide a nice touch to this clean looking stairway.

Talavera tile-faced risers are in alternating patterns and solids with *saltillo* treads. This is a second floor landing with a stairway to the roof deck.

Talavera treads with a sawtooth pattern on the riser face.

This stairway, as are many in Mexico, is without handrails. One gets used to this fact soon after ascending for the first time. The black treads are painted wood.

CHAPTER

9

Fireplaces

This fireplace with clean lines is on a raised hearth with the wooden mantel offset to the right and wrapping the edge of the chimney.

The fireplace opening is raised and framed with ceramic tile. A non-combustible hearth is a good idea where you have a wood-burning fireplace.

A raised hearth, cantilevered to provide additional seating, wraps around the fireplace opening. A wrap-around *cantera* mantel is supported by two *cantera* monkey figures.

This elongated fireplace with a slightly raised hearth has two *cantera* columns supporting the huge wooden mantel.

The uniquely designed fireplace, with cone-shaped flue, is flanked by built-in, rounded seating.

A concrete finish is on this fireplace with a wrap-around *cantera* hearth and mantel. Many gas-fired fireplaces do not have flues.

This fireplace is in an indoor patio.

The *cantera* appears as an application to an existing wall to frame the fireplace.

The hood is the primary feature of this fireplace.

A fireplace shape reminiscent of those used by Southwest American Indians.

Beautiful marble frames this fireplace.

A gas-fired fireplace shares the wall with a series of bookshelves.

Here is an architect-designed fireplace with an off-center hearth and mantel. The figures on them were collected during the owners' world-wide travels.

This classical fireplace is used as a planter when not in use.

Built into a corner, this fireplace has a curved hearth and *cantera* mantel.

Another fireplace built into a corner, with a cone-shaped hood and a mantel.

This *cantera*-framed fireplace has two columns supporting the mantel.

A raised, cantilevered hearth and firebox rest on massive cantera columns that were designed for this house.

The raised, wrap-around, concrete hearth was built to support the brick firebox and wooden mantel.

A rustic look is achieved in stone with a raised hearth and wooden mantel. The stone work has brick sections on edge forming a herringbone pattern inside the firebox.

Corner fireplaces are appropriate when space is scarce. This is a flue-less, gas-powered design.

The fireplace wall in this bedroom has a green ceramic "pineapple" that was made in Michoacan.

Individual color tiles frame this fireplace and reflect the ceiling finish, where instead of tile, a painted tile look-a-like was created.

The raise hearth of *cantera* wraps the fire box. The fire box contains stacked brick.

This corner fireplace is raised above book shelves.

CHAPTER

10

Lighting

A Moroccan metal and glass light fixture reflects the owners' worldly travels.

Just inside the entry doors, this electric chandelier has an old world design.

This light fixture is a perforated metal design made locally.

A contemporary light fixture hangs over the center of the kitchen, lighting the breakfast table.

A twelve-light, candle-like chandelier illuminates the dining table.

A Moroccan hanging light is compatible with old Mexican building designs.

This thirty-two light chandelier conveys the European roots in Mexican interior design.

A typical wall light, this Old World style is found on many interior and exterior house walls.

This lighting fixture has a shape often found in Mexican kitchens where direct light is needed the most.

This fixture is pyramid shaped and installed with the apex down, reflecting upward. It is suitable for lighting a two-story ceiling.

This contemporary spun aluminum shade was originally a hanging fixture in an old Esprit store in San Diego. It was adapted for track lighting in this Mexican home.

A simple, half-barrel-shaped wire enclosure attaches to the wall over any standard light bulb.

A large glass globe that originally hung in an Esprit store in San Diego was adapted to serve as a table lamp.

Perforated metal bent in a circular shape makes a sconce with a unique design.

Far left:
This beveled glass and metal frame fixture is reminiscent of similar designs from Morocco and it gives an Old World look to Mexican interiors.

Left:
An old-time oil lamp hangs over a living room.

A hanging Victorian lamp with dangling, cut-glass prisms lights a kitchen.

An inverted fabric cone hangs next to a fireplace.

This colorful leaded and stained glass ceiling fixture was made by the owner of this Mexican home.

This Old World-style glass and metal fixture is appropriate in Mexican home interiors.

CHAPTER

11

Ceilings & Floors

This ceiling was painted to reflect the tile surrounding the fireplace in the room.

This herringbone-patterned ceiling, made by using a standard-size, *saltillo* paver, was installed over the plywood forms before the cement roof slab was poured in place. The discoloration occurs from seepage of the wet concrete during curing.

In this ceiling, rectangular *saltillo* pavers form a standard rectangular pattern. The pavers were laid on top of the plywood forms prior to pouring the concrete slab.

When this hip roof was built, the forms were installed flush with the top of the intersecting large timbers, and the wood strips were laid on top of the forms before the concrete roof was poured in place.

Bamboo strips were installed as a finish texture after the concrete roof had been poured in place.

Cut granite squares make an interesting pattern in this exterior floor.

A universal use of *saltillo* tile with small pebbles in-filled with the grout.

Cantera pavers with larger pebbles embedded in the grout.

The is a sample of the wood flooring in one of the local, 300-year-old churches.

With the right kind of equipment, *saltillo* is putty in the hands of an artisan. This detail is one example of different patterns coming together.

Concrete walk with steel troweled perimeter.

This tiled floor has three styles of tile that meet at a step where the edge of the sculpted tile meets the solid gray.

A combination of pavers and cobblestones make this floor pattern.

Saltillo tiles and a *talavera* tile meet at an intersection with marble-sized spheres to add an interesting design element.

A floor pattern of *café* tiles with *roja* squares and *negra* circles.

A tiled floor pattern that combines rectangular *saltillo* tiles with a *daysi roja* square.

This tiled floor design is similar to the "Seville" pattern.

CHAPTER 12

Architectural Details

This interesting design is a wrought iron railing insert.

Mounted on this plain wall is an intriguing iron design symbol.

Many pieces of wood were combined to build this door that has strips of metal holding the pieces together.

Cantera cut stone surrounds and embellishes this doorway.

An intricate design is carved into this well-made entry door.

Roof detail and archway using sculpted concrete at a contemporary house in the *compo*.

Detail of a clamshell window made with sculpted concrete.

The main entry door detail.

A large *cupola* roof structure serves as a skylight to the room below.

A curved element has added interest to this otherwise straight wrought iron railing. The glass blocks in the floor provide additional daylight to the room below.

The typical masonry construction is found in San Miguel. Notice the bands of concrete, both vertical and horizontal, that provide strength to the structure, while the bricks are non-load-bearing. Because other buildings are expected to be built adjacent to them, these walls will not be finished like the white walls visible on the second floor.

One wall has a recessed hole with a pivoting wood-framed window.

A pair of half-round handles forms a circle on this double garage door.

Double hand pulls on this old door use two halves to form a cross when the doors are closed.

This is the answer to an age old problem…what to do about rain water on the roof. Here a simple concrete scupper drops the water into the garden below.

Here the void produces the address number 8.

A hand-carved wooden wall unit represents contemporary craftsmanship.

Chairs handmade by Mexican artisans in the San Miguel area.

Examples of contemporary hand carving in furniture constructed in the San Miguel area.

A hand-carved panel.

Hand carved-drawer fronts for a chest.

Glossary

Agua. Water
A la derecha. To the right
Alberca. Pool
Amigo. Friend
Arboles. Trees
Arcada. Arcade
Armario. Cabinet
Arquitecto. Architect
Artes. Arts
Azul. Blue
Azulejo. Tile

Balaustrada. Balustrade
Banco. Bench
Bandidos. Bandits
Baño. Bathroom
Boveda. Vault
Brasero. Brazier

Canalon. Gutter
Cantera. Volcanic stone
Cantina. Bar
Cartas. Letters
Casa. House
Cascada. Waterfall
Casita. Small house
Chimenea. Fireplace
Clavo. Nail
Cobalto. Colbalt
Cochera. Garage
Cocina. Kitchen
Comedor. Dining room
Comoda. Chest of drawers
Compo. Away from town
Cornisa. Cornice
Corredor. Corridor
Cristo. Christ
Cupula. Cupola or dome

Entrada. Entryway
Equipal. Pigskin furniture
Escalera. Stairway or ladder

Fabrica. Fabricate
Fachada. Facade
Flores. Flowers
Fuenta. Fountain

Hierro. Iron
Hombre. Man

Iglesia. Church
Iluminacion. Lighting

Jardin. Garden
Jarrones. Large jars

Laja. Flat rock
Llamador. Door

Nicho. Niche

Ojo. Eye

Petateyes. Reed mats
Petatillo. A thin brick
Pilar. Pillar
Portal. Foyer
Portico. Covered porch at entry
Porton. Large door
Postigo. Small door usually inside another door
Puerta. Door

Que Pasa. What's happening

Recamara. Bedroom
Reja. Iron grating or railing
Retablo. Religious painting

Sala. Living room
Saltillo. Floor tile, generally fired, sometime not.
Santo. Saint
Silla. Chair
Sillon. Couch

Tablero. Panel of tiles
Talavera. Hand-painted, twice fired, tin-glazed earthen ware
Troje. Wooden house

Vestibulo. Hall or public lobby
Viga. Beam or girder

Zaguan. Passage from street to inner courtyard
Zocalo. Baseboard

Resources

The following resources are either in San Miguel proper or outside the town's perimeter, but within the greater metropolitan area.

Food & Tabletop

Bonanza
Mesones 43
152 1260
A complete in-town supermarket with hard-to-find imported ítems.

De Talavera
Puebla No. 60 esq.
Tamaulipas
Delores Hidalgo, Gto.
(418) 182 0749
An extensive line of *talavera* dinnerware.

La Buena Vida
Hernandez Macias 72
152 2211
Bakery & Cafe
Natural whole grain breads, French baguettes and unique pastries.

La Europea
Canal 13
152 2003
An extensive selection of wines and spirits.

Maxi Vinos
Zacateros 86
152 2219
A good selection of wines and spirits.

Petitfour
Mesones 99
154 4010
Pastry shop, bar and café. Homemade chocolates, cakes, pies and French pastries.

Furniture

Arden Casa de Muebles
Libr. Celaya a Delores 26
154 8010
Furniture and home decor accessories.

Camila
Sollano 30
152 2697
Antique furniture, etched glass,custom made linens & table cloths.

Casa Canal
Canal 3
152 0479
Hand-carved furniture.

Casa del Inquisidor
Aldama 1
154 6868
Household accessories and an extensive hardware selection.

Casa Marie Luisa
Ancha San Antonio 26
152 2983
Furniture and home decor accessories.

Coba Art Décor
Juarez 7
154 7516
Interior design, accessories and fine furniture from India.

Colección Cuatro Vientos
Sollano 31
154 9132
Furniture and home decor accessories.

C. Dewayne Youts
Fabrica la Aurora
152 5481
Manufacturing of wood and iron furniture, 17th century reproductions, custom kitchens andaccessories.

El Progresso
Rancho Sta. Clara
(418) 120 3106
Hand-crafted furniture.

Evos
Hernandez Macias 55
152 0813
Classic San Miguel style home furnishings, Spanish Colonial furniture, importedsofas, upholstered furniture & fabrics and oriental rugs.

Finca
Fabrica la Aurora
154 8323
Furniture, accessories and interiors.

Hacienda la Diligencia
Hernandez Macias 118
152 1626
Custom furniture made to your design and specifications.

Manuel Padron
Santa Clara
progresso2004@prodigy.com.mx
Hand-crafted furniture.

Marcia Bland Brown
Hacienda Calderón
044 415 153 3176
Furniture design & manufacturing, antiques, interior & architectural design and restoration.

Namuh Collection
Camino Alcocer Km 2.2
154 8080
Indoor/outdoor furniture and accessories from Asia.

SHOPS

Antigua Casa Canela
Umaran 20
152 1880
Antiques, Colonial art and home décor accessories.

Artes de México
Calzada de la Aurora 47
152 0764
Mexican arts and crafts, tin ornaments, Colonial furniture and folk art.

ArtesMéxico
Zacateros 81A
154 8531
Quality hand-wrought copper.

Azulejos Talavera Cortes S.A.de C.V.
Aldama No. 18
Delores Hidalgo, C.I.N., GTO.,
México
(418) 182 1168
Finest glazed *talavera* tiles for floor finishing as well as an infinite range of accessories.

Buenas Noches
Fabrica la Aurora
154 9624
Fine bed and bath furnishings.

Cantadora
Fabrica la Aurora
154 8302
Cantera, fireplaces, columns, door frames and decorative accessories.

Carrillo Vertix Hermanos
Puebla No. 54
Delores Hidalgo, C.I.N., GTO.,
México
(418) 182 0122
Talavera tiles, traditional & Barcelona, murals & accessories.

Casa Coloniales
Canal 36
152 0286
Furniture, upholstery, fabrics, trim, pillows, spreads, curtains, rugs, chandeliers, sconces, stone ornaments, and gifts.

Casa Roberto
Libr. a Queretaro 35
152 8620
Lighting, ceiling fans, water filters, purifiers, radiant heaters and fireplace accessories.

Galería Tesoro
Recreo 8B
154 5595
Folk art and home decor accessories.

Icpalli
Correo 43
152 1236
Fabric for interior design, window treatment, furniture and home accessories.
.
Icons
Pila Seca 3
152 5762
Traditional Byzantine images.

Ilunina San Miguel
Calzada de la Luz 51
154 7643
Commercial & residential lighting,chandeliers, lamps and sconces.

Lan Art
Ancha de San Antonio
152 1566
Rugs, bedspreads, pillows and household accessories.

La Victoriana
Hernandez Macias 72
152 6903
Botanical beauty products, herbal and homeopathic remedies, flower essence and aromatherapy.

La Zandunga
H Macias 129
152 4608
Fine Mexican rugs.

Mitu Atelier
Sollano 32
044 415 117 9431
Home accessories, custom furniture and antiques.

Productos Herco, S.A.
Relox #12
152 1434
A large selection of faucets, sinks, bathtubs in various materials including copper and marble, decorative hardware and kitchen accessories.

Sisal
Fabrica la Aurora
154 8944
Home decor and interior design.

Sollano 16
Sollano 16
154 8872
Lifestyle & home décor and accessories.

Talavera Vázquez
Puebla No. 56
Delores Hidalgo, C.I.N., GTO.,
México
(418) 182 2914
Talavera tiles, flowerpots, murals and earthenware.

Zocalo
Hernandez Macias 110
152 0663
Fine Mexican folk art and furniture and hand-blown glassware.

Booksellers

Biblioteca Publica
Insurgentes 25
152 3770
Books, posters, guide books, gift items, cook books.

Casa de Papel
Mesones 57
154 5187
Greeting cards, journals, photo albums, candles, guide books, road maps, Mexican cook books, prints, posters and CDs.

El Colibri
Sollano 30
152 0751
Spanish language books, art books and artists' materials.

El Pato
M Ledesma 19
152 1543
Art supplies, design & accessories.

Libreria la Deriva
Fabrica de la Aurora
Art books, English and Spanish language books.

Garrison & Garrison
Hernandez Macias 59
152 4547
New & second-hand books.

Lagundi
Umaran 17
152 0830
Art supplies, frames and framing, posters, original prints, books and magazines.

Libros El Tecolote
Jesús 11
152 7395
English language books, Mexican history, literature, art & design books.

Wearable Art

Barbara Porter
Zacateros 47
152 7463
Fashion designs for men & women.

Black & White
Loreto 20
154 4493
Traveling clothes, Alpaca sweaters and accessories.

Caracol Collection
Cuadrante 30
152 1617
Fine and applied art, furniture, arte copper and ceramics.

Christofas
Cuadrante 2
154 9392
Unique designer jewelry, sculpture, décor art, mobiles and gemstones.

Creación Marcela Andre
San Francisco 7
154 9868
Original art, jewelry and decorations.

Diva
Hernandez Macias 72
152 4980
Jewelry, accessories and creative quality clothes in European linens.

Girasol
Sn Francisco 72
152 2734
Mexican casuals.

Goldie Designs
Zacateros 19
154 7521
Classic clothing, elegant jewelry and custom accessories.

Nuevo México
Aparicio 1
152 4510
Navajo style crafts.

7th Heaven
Sollano 13
154 4677
Unique jewelry, art, gifts and clothes.

Galleries

Akitsch
Pila Seca 16A
152 7343
Funky & kitsch jewelry, accessories & decoration.

Atenea Gallery
Jesús 2
152 0785
Paintings, sculpture, graphics, jewelry and art objects.

Azul Y Plata Disenos
Cuna de Allende 15
154 8192
Jewelry.

Casa Diana Art Gallery
Recreo 48
152 0885
Contemporary art.

Edgar Soberon
San Francisco 66
152 0306
Painting studio.

Estudio Ezcurdia
Fabrica de la Aurora
152 6539
Paintings.

Galleria Anna Julia Agudo
Plaza Principal 18
Cell: 103 0228
Latin American art & contemporary paintings.

Galería Aspen
Mesones 74
154 4441
Investment art.

Gallery Atotonilco
185 2225
Exceptional Mexican folk art, historic photos, vintage textiles.

Generator Gallery
Fabrica la Aurora
154 9588
Contemporary artists.

Galería Izamal
Mesones 80
154 5409
Paintings and jewelry design by local artists.

Galería Mariposa
Recreo 36
152 4488
Specializing in one-of-a-kind pieces by the great masters of Mexican folk art.

Galería Pérgola
Instituto Allende
154 5595
Mexican fine art.

Mero
Zacateros 24
154 8580
Contemporary art.

Yam gallery
Institute Allende
Ancha de San Antonio
152 0338
Art + Design.

ZOHO
Fabrica de la Aurora
152 4791
A contemporary art gallery

Services

Fortuna
Pila Seca 3
152 7782
Conservation & preservation of fine art, photographs, textiles and memorabilia.

Information

Atencion
Insurgentes 25
152 3770
Weekly newspaper.

Promocion Mexican Culture
Hidalgo 18
152 0121

Tourist Information
Plaza Principal 10
120 4520

Bibliography

Barragan, The Complete Works. New York: Princeton Architectural Press, 1996.

de Haro, Fernando and Omar Fuentes. *Arquitectos Mexicanos, Una Visipn Contemporanea.* México D.F. Arquitectos Mexicanos Editores S.A. de C.V., 2004.

------. *Mexican Interiors: Style & Personality*. México D.F.: Arquitectos Mexicanos Editores S.A. de C.V.,2003.

Levick, Melba and Gina Hyams. *Mexicasa, The Enchanting Inns and Haciendas of Mexico*. San Francisco: Chronicle Books, 2001.

------. *In a Mexican Garden: Courtyards, Pools, and Open-Air Living Rooms.* San Francisco: Chronicle Books, 2005.

Levick, Melba, Tony Cohan and Masako Takahashi. *Mexicolor: The Spirit of Mexican Design.* San Francisco: Chronicle Books, 1998.

Luscombe-Whyte, Mark and Dominic Bradbury. *Mexico Architecture, Interiors & Design.* New York: Harper Collins Publishers, 2004.

Stoeltie, Barbara and Rene Stoeltie. *Living in Mexico: Vivre au Mexique:* Cologne: Taschen, 2004.

Streeter-Porter, Tim. *Casa Mexicana: The Architecture, Design and Style of Mexico.* New York: Stewart, Tabori & Chang, 1994.

Streeter-Porter, Tim, and Annie Kelly. *Casa Mexicana Style*. New York: Stewart, Tabori & Chang, 2006.

Villela, Khristaan, Ellen Bradbury and Logan Wagner. *Contemporary Mexican Design and Architecture.* Layton, Utah: Gibbs Smith, Publisher, 2002.

Yampolsky, Mariana and Chloe Sayer. *The Traditional Architecture of Mexico.* New York: Thames and Hudson, 1993.

Ypma, Herbert. *Mexican Contemporary.* New York: Stewart, Tabori & Chang, 1997.